JOEL

a book for
- those affected by natural disasters
- those afraid of the future

**A MINI-COMMENTARY
ON THE BOOK OF JOEL
BY DAVID HEWETSON**

Scripture Union

London   Sydney   Wellington   Cape Town

JOEL
© David Hewetson
First published in 1977
Revised and reprinted 1990

All rights reserved. No portion of this publication may be reproduced by any means without the written permission of the publisher.

Scripture Union books are published by
ANZEA PUBLISHERS
3-5 Richmond Road
Homebush West, NSW 2140
Australia

ISBN 0 85892 428 5

Scripture Union UK
130 City Road
London EC1V 2NJ
England

ISBN 0 86201 685 1

Text artwork: Madeline Gianatti
Photography: NSW Agriculture & Fisheries

Printed in Singapore by
Singapore National Printers Ltd

Introduction

If a tropical cyclone smashes a town is it a message to anyone? Are disasters a punishment for sins? If so, for whose sins? Are those hit by such things *worse* sinners than others?

In the Bible the destruction of the wicked cities of the Jordon Plain (Genesis 19:17, 24–25; Amos 4:11; Luke 17:29,30) was God's judgment on them. But disobedience to God is not the only reason for disasters. The Book of Job in the Old Testament makes that clear. In it the hero, Job, is overtaken by all sorts of troubles. The friends who came to 'comfort' him offer their theories on why he is being afflicted. They think it is punishment for undisclosed sins. Job disagrees with them. And the reader must disagree too because he knows, even more than Job, what is happening. The reader knows that even though Job's sufferings are a mystery to him there *is* an explanation for them, and it is not the one offered by his friends. Since only God knows this explanation, only he can explain it.

The idea that all afflictions are punishment for sins was still very prevalent in Jesus' day (John 9:2). But Jesus did not agree with it either (John 9:3). In speaking of two local disasters (Luke 13:1–5), he insisted that those who perished in them were no worse than others. The biggest calamity for anyone, he said, is coming to God's final judgment without repenting of one's sins.

We today should get the message from *any* disaster. Any disaster is a kind of 'dress rehearsal' for Judgment Day. And this is the message that the prophet Joel also brings to us. His land had been devastated by a swarm of locusts. This, he said, was a sign that the Day of the Lord was coming and that the nation ought to be warned by it and repent.

The people must have responded to Joel's call, for in the midst of his message he changes from challenging them to praising God (2:18). God would heal their land and restore it; he would bring back its fruitfulness and prosperity. But just as the nation's earthly troubles were connected with God's great final judgment, so too their prosperity would be much more than an earthly thing. It would be part of God's final plan to save mankind and transform the world.

Joel promised his hearers that two great things would happen in the future. First, God would pour out his Spirit on the ordinary people and so bring them into a new and closer relationship to himself. This promise was taken by the first Christians as being fulfilled on the Day of Pentecost (Acts 2:15–21). Secondly, God would some day establish complete victory over all evil things. He would bring all the various forces of history into the 'valley of decision' (3:14) and overthrow all that is opposed to him.

So we learn a great deal from Joel. We learn how to interpret earthly troubles and disasters. We are reminded that they are signs of the great final crisis of world judgment. And we are reminded afresh of our need of repentance and God's Spirit to prepare us to face this crisis. In Joel we find things to sober and humble us, but also things to give us hope and encouragement. It is a most important message.

1 The doomsday army

Joel 1:1–7

Until fairly recently the most powerful weapons in the world belonged to nature. Arrows, spears and swords were as nothing compared to earthquakes, plagues and floods. Like the atom bomb and biological warfare today, these natural disasters were the doomsday weapons of the ancient world. Since people had no control over them they were, of course, God's weapons and he used them both *for* and *against* his people.

God used wind and water to make a path for his people through the Red Sea and also to destroy the Egyptian army (Exodus 14:21–29). He brought his people to their knees with a crippling drought (1 Kings 17:7). By means of a plague he humbled the world's most powerful invader right at the gates of Jerusalem (2 Kings 19:35). And in Joel's time the weapon in God's hand was a devastating plague of locusts.

To modern city dwellers, locusts perhaps do not sound too frightening. But in the Middle East a bad swarm could destroy the whole economy and jeopardise the future. In 1889 there was one such plague that spread 3,200 km over the Red Sea. It was calculated that it contained 24,420 billion locusts weighing 43,600 tonnes! In fact the island of Cyprus was made desolate between the years 1600 and 1881 until a method was found to destroy the locusts. Today in a number of places the swarms are sprayed from the air with insecticides.

So Joel does not exaggerate when he speaks of the locust plague as if it was a Doomsday army. And to him it was, since it was a sign of the Day of Judgment (see 1:15) as well as being an ordinary national disaster.

The appeal to experience (1:2–3)
Memory has a way of linking the past and the future with the present. Those who have lived in a place and those who have lived there a long time are the best judges of how remarkable any event is. The 'inhabitants of the land' and the 'aged men' knew that this locust plague was the worst that they had ever seen. And just as memory helped them with the past, they must now make it work for them in the

future by passing on their experience to coming generations (1:3). The special disaster carried a special message and it must not be forgotten.

The battle of the bugs (1:4–7)

The devastation was systematic and complete. The four kinds of locust mentioned (1:4) refer either to different species or stages of growth. Joel simply means that whatever one group left the other group destroyed. It was *total* destruction.

When the economy is smashed the luxuries, and those who love them, suffer first. The drunkards (1:5) find that the very source of their amusement has been swallowed by the locusts. Not only would there now be no money to buy wine; there would be none to buy and no way to produce it.

The locust swarm is like an invading army of incredible size (1:6). Its teeth are like those of the lion. Their numbers, their strength, their voracious appetites and razor-sharp teeth make them into a terribly efficient destruction machine. They turn their annihilating power against the two staples of Israel's economy—the vine and the fig tree (1:7). They consume everything—the fruit, the flowers, the leaves. They even gnaw the bark back to the wood! The whole landscape is eaten white like snow and the trees and shrubs, stripped of everything, take on a stark wintry look. No army of men could do more damage, nor could they so jeopardise the future as the locust army has done.

Talking points

1. Natural disasters 'were, of course, God's weapons and he used them both *for* and *against* his people'. Does this remain true today? Share any examples you can think of. See Exodus 14:21–31, 1 Kings 17:1–7, 2 Kings 19:32–35 and Matthew 24:1–8.

2. If our nation was hit by natural or economic disaster, what would you do about it?
   How do you cope with trouble when it comes upon you individually? Share some examples with one another. Is there a *right* way of coping with trouble?

3. What is the relationship between trouble and sin? See Genesis 3:16–19, 6:5–8, John 9:1–3 and Romans 2:9–10.

4. What is the relationship between trouble and God? See Job 12:13–25, Isaiah 45:6–7, John 9:1–3 and Romans 2:5–8.

5. What is the purpose of trouble? Is there any way of knowing why it happens? Some of the passages that you have already looked at will be helpful. See also Acts 5:1–11, 8:1–5, Hebrews 12:4–13 and Romans 5:3–5.

2 Lamentations unlimited

Joel 1:8–20

The frivolous drunkards have already been called to wake up and weep. Now Joel turns to the more serious-minded people. Ordinary citizens are called to lament. The priests mourn, as does the very ground itself. And the farmers must be 'confounded' and 'wail'. The grief that grips them all is as shattering as that of a young woman deeply in love but bereaved of her fiance (1:8). This was almost like losing a husband, since engagements were permanent and binding amongst the Hebrews.

The gladness-eaters (1:8–12)
The stricken land certainly looks as though it is in mourning (1:10), like the grieving people. The fields and the land are often personalised in the Old Testament, either as rejoicing (see Psalm 65:12–13) or being in anguish (as here). The priests are particularly distressed (1:9), since the ruin of the fields means that there is no offering for the regular morning and evening sacrifices (Exodus 29:38–42). The absence of these tokens of fellowship with the Lord makes the people feel that his presence and favours have been taken from them.

So the locusts devour spiritual as well as material things! They are a Doomsday army through which God speaks in a way that the people are forced to understand. The people have neglected God (though not their religious rituals); now they must experience his absence and what it is like when 'gladness fails'.

Because God is a God of love, there is mercy in his judgments. When our sins rob us of gladness, God can use that to bring us back to himself in repentance. The very results of our neglect can be a chastening rod in his hand to bring us to a better mind.

Everybody pray (1:13–20)

The Temple services have been spoiled by the locust plague. But people can still pray; indeed that is all they can do now. And in this the priests (1:13) must give a lead. For not only do they have the task of interceding for the people, they are also their teachers and examples in spiritual things. And if the people have neglected God, then it may well be because of the carelessness of the priests in their own devotion or concern for them. People who have a ministry in the church, and that includes every Christian, have a double responsibility—for themselves and for others. Keeping themselves in spiritual order is an important part of what they do for others.

The priests, dressed in sackcloth, will mourn all night at the shrine. Then they must get the people together and call them to national repentance. They must all fast (1 Kings 21:9; Zechariah 7:3–5), for fasting and sackcloth were outward signs of their penitence and concern. It is easy to make rituals like this formal and mechanical, and to imagine that somehow or other they impress God and win his favour. But with Joel they were a sign of earnestness. They must 'cry to the Lord' (1:14). There must be genuine humility, confession of sin, a plea for his forgiveness and the renewal of their relationship with him.

The locusts were bad enough. But to Joel they were only a sign of a calamity far more terrible. The awful destruction they caused was only a token of the far more devastating 'destruction from the Almighty' (1:15) that would come with the approaching 'Day of the Lord'.

How the land is now suffering! All the joy has gone out of worship (1:16). Even nature seems to conspire with the locusts to increase the anguish (1:17). The cattle recognise their plight (1:18). Even the wild beasts (1:20) seem to lift up their eyes to heaven and beg for help. If only *men* would show as much sense and cry to the Lord to forgive their sins and heal their land!

Perhaps Joel despaired of his people. Perhaps he simply wanted to practise what he has been preaching about prayer. In any case he too begins to cry to the Lord (1:19)—no doubt not merely about the locust plague but about God's final judgment of the world. He knew that when real calamities overtake us at the personal, national or even at the international level, the only path of action is prayer. But he also knew that, no matter how severe these calamities, they are but dress rehearsals for the last great world crisis—the judgment of God. To be unready for *that day* is the greatest disaster of all (Matthew 24:42)!

Talking points

1. While millions of people around the world are in want, Australians spend millions of dollars in gambling, liquor, entertainment and other luxuries. What do you consider to be luxuries? How would you react if they were taken away? See Joel 1:5, Matthew 6:19–21, 7:25–33 and 19:21–22.

2. What responsibilities do Christians have for the spiritual state of their nation? How ought we exercise those responsibilities? See Joel 1:14 and 2 Chronicles 7:13–14.

3. Of what does our nation need to repent? What would you expect to result from repentance on a national scale?

4. How important is prayer to you? Is it really a priority? How important is prayer to your relationship with God? Why is it important for Christians to be—individually and corporately—prayerful people? See John 16:24, Philippians 4:6–7, James 5:13–18 and 1 John 5:14–15.

5. What should a lack of joy in our service to Christ say to us? How is it possible for Christians to be joyful and thankful in all situations? Compare Job 10:18–22 with John 16:24, Philippians 4:4 and 1 Thessalonians 5:16–18.

3   First the bad news . . .

Joel 2:1–11

Does God speak through disasters? This is a question we have already asked. And we have suggested that they can be general reminder of the final crisis of God's judgment. But some disasters, like Joel's locust plague, carried a *special* message. In these God actually shouted his warnings to the people, perhaps because they had been too deaf to hear him speaking in other ways.

So here (2:11) God is at the head of *his* locust army, calling out a warning to his people. Joel's message is simple and ominous—the Day of the Lord is not only terrible; it is close and coming fast. Those responsible for the people's welfare must also sound a warning in Zion (2:1), the spiritual centre of the nation. And the people must respond to it earnestly and sincerely. They must not trifle with God by simply offering him more temple sacrifices. They must come before him and 'tremble'.

The Day of the Lord (2:1)

Perhaps you have been wondering what this term 'the Day of the Lord' actually means? It is an important one in the Bible. We have already met it in 1:15. It is mentioned twice (2:1,11) in the section we are now studying and we shall meet it again in 2:31 and 3:14.

People in the Old Testament did not believe that this present age of the world would last forever. It was so spoiled by sin and suffering that it could not really be repaired. Instead it would be replaced by a golden age of peace and joy and righteousness (Hosea 2:18).

The end of this age and the beginning of the new one was called 'the Day of the Lord'. It would be entirely *God's* day, when he would be exalted (Isaiah 2:11) and victorious over all that was opposed to him. Though he had always been king, the evils of the present age made it possible for men to forget him and even to defy him. But on that day his reign would be recognised by all and, with the removal of all evil, perfectly established.

It was easy for God's people to presume on this. They knew that he would overthrow those that opposed him and so vindicate his people against those who accused and afflicted them. But Amos (Amos 5:18–20) and other prophets reminded them that God would judge all sin, including their own, if they were disobedient and rebellious.

Jesus announced that the Kingdom of God had come (Mark 1:14–15) and his miracles were signs (Luke 7:22, 11:20) that the new age was present in power. The gift of the Spirit at Pentecost was to make this fact quite unmistakable. What must have surprised his first hearers, however, was that the old age did not immediately pass away, nor did the new age come in all its power. We live in both ages (1 Corinthians 10:11) and, though we have tasted of the good things to come, we must still wait for them to come in all their fullness. This will be at Christ's return. Then the Day of the Lord will become the '*day of Jesus Christ*' (Philippians 1:6,10; 2 Thessalonians 2:2).

Dark days (2:2–11)

Since the Day of the Lord will be the end of history as we know it, it will be (from one point of view) the greatest calamity of all time. It will be a day of darkness and clouds and gloom (2:2).

But locusts also darken the sky (cf. Exodus 10:14–15). Those who have seen them say that they are often massed so thickly that they shut out the rays of the sun. This made them for Joel an excellent sign that the Day of the Lord was near. The locust plague was not itself that great day but it was its forerunner (cf. Revelation 9:2–3) and it had many things in common with the day. It was an unparalleled disaster (2:2) and, as such, spoke loudly of the end of all things. It was as inescapable (2:3) as the judgment of God. It would result in the very annihilation of the beauty and harmony of God's original creation; of Eden.

The locusts are now described (2:4–9) as an invading army. The head of the locust has a strange resemblance to that of the horse (2:4; cf. Revelation 9:7). In both the Italian and German languages this is what locusts are actually called (e.g. the German is 'hay horse'). Horses in the Old Testament are symbols of war and of human power opposed to God (Isaiah 31:1–3). So the locusts are 'warhorses' (2:4), whose approach is like the sound of chariots (2:5; see also Revelation 9:9) or crackling flames.

This swarm is said to come from the north (2:20). For people in Jerusalem this would be seen first upon the mountains (2:5) like an army poised to swoop. The people look up in terror (2:6) as the locust army charges (2:7a), hurling itself against the city. They are relentless (2:7b) and behave like a regular disciplined force (2:8). They are inescapable. They find their way into every part of the city, even inside houses through the open unglazed windows (2:9). Though, of course, all these things do accurately describe an actual locust plague, Joel is really saying that the *Day of the Lord* will be like this—terrifying, relentless and inescapable.

God's day will shake the earth (2:10) and dim the stars (Isaiah 13:10; Matthew 24:29). Though his voice is now heard at the head of a mere army of locusts, in a limited local way as the instrument of his word (2:11), God's real message to Israel (and to us) is that his final day of reckoning is great, terrible and unable to be endured.

Talking points

1. 'They must not trifle with God by simply offering him more temple sacrifices. They must come before him and *tremble*.' Are we guilty of being too familiar with God? Should we tremble before God? In terms of your relationship with God, what does it mean to tremble before him? See Joel 2:10–11, Psalm 96:9 and Philippians 2:12–13.

2. In what ways do you 'presume' upon God? Do you take his goodness towards you for granted? What does Job 2:1–10 have to say about such things?

3. Do you think as much as you should about the end of the world and the return of Jesus Christ? What differences would it make to your lifestyle if you did? See Romans 13:11–14.

4. How can we share our concern about the coming Day of the Lord? Would people consider us 'alarmists' if we spoke more of it? (Remember, ecologists are not afraid to warn us of the doom which awaits us all if we fail to conserve the earth.)

5. According to Joel 2:1–11, Mark 1:14–15 and 1 Corinthians 10:11 how is the age in which we live different from the age in which Joel lived?

4 Now, perhaps . . . some good news

Joel 2:12–17

All preachers and prophets hope for the best. Even when they preach doom, they long that men will repent and God forgive. They warn of destruction but hope for the possibility of God's blessing, saying, 'Who knows?' (2:14).

Torn hearts (2:12–14)

It was now late for repentance but perhaps not too late. Judgment had already begun to roll across the land in the form of the locust plague. 'Yet even now', said Joel, repentance (2:12) might change the whole situation (2 Samuel 24:15–25). But it would have to be a deep sincere return to the Lord done with 'all the heart' (and in the Bible 'heart' denotes will and mind, not just affection or emotion). There would be an outward expression of this inward change through such things as fasting, weeping and mourning. But the heart (2:13) must also be 'broken' (Psalm 51:17). Rather than tear their outer garments (cf. Jeremiah 36:24–25), the people themselves must be inwardly torn with sorrow and regret.

The basis of this eleventh-hour hope of forgiveness was not merely human optimism; it was a deepened understanding of God's character. Moses had first understood him as full of love, mercy and kindness (Exodus 34:6 ff), and Israel had had good cause to testify to this again and again (Psalm 86:15; Jonah 4:2). The Old Testament also looked forward to better things still, to a new age of grace when God's love would creatively mend broken relationships between men and himself. With this confidence then, Joel was able to say 'Who knows?' Perhaps God will save the land from total destruction by the locusts and so leave behind a blessing (2:14a). There would not only be food for the people but, as a result of this, an offering (2:14b). This would be a concrete way for them to say 'thank you' to the Lord for his grace and mercy.

Cancel the honeymoon (2:15–17)

For the third time Joel calls everybody (2:15) to penitential prayer (see also 1:14 and 2:1). But this time he tells them what they (through the priests) shall say (2:17). No one is excused from this prayer meeting. All those who would normally be exempt—the aged, the infants, even the honeymooners—must come. (See Deuteronomy 20:7 and 24:5 for the newly-weds' exemption from other activities.)

The priests, like Moses of old, have the task of mediating between God and the people (Deuteronomy 9:25ff). Their prayer is to be simple and direct. It is based on the clear teaching of the Old Testament that the only way to deal with sin is to cast oneself on the mercy of God and implore him to spare his people (2:17). Gifts will not buy his favour; sacrifices will not change his mind. Humility and repentance alone open the way for him to show grace and mercy, and only then by way of thanksgiving can gifts (2:14) be brought.

The priests' plea for mercy is to be based on God's honour. When his people, bound to him by the convenant relationship, become a 'byword' among unbelievers (2:17b), his name suffers with theirs. Looking at the catastrophe facing God's people, even unbelievers are able to question the existence of God. 'Where is their God?' they say contemptuously. This is part of the great responsibility of belonging to God. But it is also the best basis on which to cry to him for mercy—not because we are in trouble, certainly not because we deserve his help, but because it is a hideous thought that *he* should be blamed for the mess we have made of things.

Have you ever wondered what might happen if God's people turned to him with all their hearts—if right across the nation or just in your local church they came together in great urgency with torn hearts and penitential words? If, wounded by the contempt in which unbelievers often hold the church, Christians called on God to show them mercy, not for their own sakes but for the sake of his honour and majesty? What would happen? As Joel hopefully puts it, 'Who knows?'

Talking points

1. What does repentance with 'all the heart' or a 'torn' heart involve? How would this kind of repentance be demonstrated in everyday life? In what ways does your life reveal such repentance? See Joel 2:12–13.

2. Read Joel 2:12–14. Discuss the meaning and implications of Joel 2:14b.

3. Read Luke 7:36–50. Discuss the following statement as it relates to this passage: 'All are equally sinful, but some are more sinful than others.'

4. The Bible clearly tells us that God is full of 'love, mercy and kindness' (e.g., 1 John 4:7–10; James 5:11 etc.). Does your experience of God confirm this biblical truth? Give reasons or examples to support your response.

5. How conscious are you that your behaviour may or may not be honouring to God? In what ways do you show that you take this responsibility seriously? See Joel 2:17, Hebrews 13:18 and 1 Peter 2:12, 13–15.

5 God the restorer

Joel 2:18–27

Can the past be undone? Can our mistakes be repaired? If we repent of our sins can God patch up the damage done to ourselves and to others? Well, things can certainly never be as if nothing had ever happened. Our characters are impaired by sin. And sometimes, for example, health or home can be so damaged that they refuse to heal. There are memories that are very hard to erase. Some people will never entirely trust us again after we have treated them badly.

And yet God *can* repair our lives. His forgiveness completely reinstates us and puts us on a par with his most obedient servants. Sometimes failure is the only cure for our proud self-confidence, the only thing that will make us throw ourselves on God's mercy and power. Perhaps too at the end God's grace will change our shame and tears into something uniquely beautiful. As C.S. Lewis said in *The Great Divorce*, (Geoffrey Bles, 1946) page 62, heaven 'works backwards' to touch with glory everything we have ever been or done.

He really cares (2:18–23)

So Joel is able to promise God's people, now repentant, that their devastated land will be restored. His past tenses in verses 18–19 show that God is already at work on this and so it is as good as done! Actually there are two sides to God's activity.

(a) His *jealousy*. This is an emotion which can hardly be entrusted to sinful men, except perhaps in a married person's right to expect an exclusive commitment from the other partner (2 Corinthians 11:2). With God it describes his strong personal feelings about his people, about good and evil and truth and falsehood (cf. Exodus 20:5). He is not detached in these matters; he is involved. He cares deeply about how people live and what they believe—especially about himself. So he cannot tolerate the arrogant contempt of the pagan nations for either the plight of his people (2:17b) or his own control of history.

(b) His *pity* or compassion. This is the other side of his deep concern, the part that actively works to help heal men. Compassion would reverse all the disasters so far described by Joel about which the people had cried to God in prayer. The staple crops were already partly restored (2:19) but there are better things still to come. The reproach or contempt of the nations (2:17b) will be removed. And more important still, so will the locusts (2:20).

Joel refers to them as 'the northerner'. Actually locusts usually come upon Palestine from the south and south east, though it is not impossible for them to come from the north. However, the word 'north' is probably used here as a symbol for that direction from which mysterious, dark, ominous forces came upon Israel (cf. Ezekiel 38:6; Isaiah 14:13). Jeremiah had already prophesied a great evil from that direction (Jeremiah 1:14, 4:6) which would later be identified as the Babylonians. We have already seen Joel using local events (i.e. the locust plague) to describe things beyond history (i.e. the Day of the Lord). He seems to be doing that here. And the good news is that this almost super-human evil, which had come upon his people, will be swept off the face of the map.

Locust swarms come and go with great suddenness. It is usually the wind that removes them and, as here (2:20), drives them into the Eastern (Dead) Sea, the Western (Mediterranean) Sea or into the 'parched and desolate land' (the desert). A shifting wind on the high Palestinian watershed could easily remove them quickly and, as has happened often enough, they are drowned and washed up on the beaches to cause an awful stench and sometimes disease. But the good thing is that they are completely removed.

Repairing the past (2:24–27)

A song of praise to the Lord must now go up from all who have suffered so badly—the land (2:21), the beasts, nature (2:22) and the people themselves (2:23). All the damage described in chapter 1 is now to be restored. The lamentation that was expressed than by all creation must be replaced with a cry of joy and praise that 'the Lord has done great things'.

For God has not only removed the destroyer—he will now restore fertility (2:22) to the devasted trees and vines. He will 'green' the land by sending upon it the life-giving rains. The early rain (2:23), which comes in October and November at the beginning of the wet season, prepares the land for seed sowing. It comes, says Joel, as a 'vindication' or a token that God's blessing has been restored to his penitent people. The latter rain in March and April at the end of the wet season will nourish and ripen the plants, and assure the people that everything is once again 'as before'—back to normal.

The renewal of the land is like a *sacrament* to God's people. It is a sign and an assurance of God's loving care and protection restored to them. They will now have a prosperity (2:24) which will more than make up for all the bad times they have been through (2:25). And the memory of the lean years will so contrast with the joy of the present that they will be moved to praise the Lord (2:26) for the ways in which he has dealt 'wondrously' with them. The shame (2:26b and 27b) that they have felt because of the contempt of the surrounding nations (2:17b) will be entirely removed. And not just by prosperity. Their fellowship with the Lord 'in the midst' of them, and their convictions about his absolute uniqueness and supremacy (2:27), will finally drive away all their former feelings of fear and shame. They will be completely restored—make no mistake about it.

Can God do that for people today? Can he make up to them all the years wasted by sin and neglect? *Of course* he can. Jesus Christ died and rose again so that we might be brought into a full and unhindered relationship with God, no matter what sort of a mess we have made of the past. When we come to him, ashamed and repentant, he restores us. As we realise his majesty (that he is our God and there is no-one else like him) and his love (that he is our deliverer and is with us), then our shame and regret is swallowed up by peace and joy. And even if we have earned the contempt of others by the way we have lived, our new and obvious fellowship with the Lord becomes such a reality that even their accusations lose their power. What a great restorer he is!

Talking points

1. Does sin permanently affect our lives? Does God's forgiveness remove its effects as well as its guilt? See Joel 2:21–27, Romans 6:1–11 and 1 John 1:9.

2. Do you find it easy to forgive others when they have wronged you? How might such forgiveness be demonstrated? See Matthew 6:9–15 and 2 Corinthians 2:5–11.

3. What does God mean when he describes himself as 'jealous'? How do you respond to this aspect of the revealed character of God? See Exodus 20:4–5, 34:13–14, Numbers 25:6–11 and 1 Corinthians 10:19–22.

4. 'The renewal of the land is like a *sacrament* to God's people. It is a sign and an assurance of God's loving care and protection restored to them.' As Christians, should we expect material well-being to accompany God's forgiveness or are our blessings only those of Ephesians 1:3? See also Joel 2:25–26 and 1 Peter 4:12–14.

5. Joel 2:27 is made real to the Israelites by the restoration of their land. How are Christians, both corporately and individually, able to experience a similar hope? See Romans 8:23–28, 2 Corinthians 3:4–18 and Ephesians 1:13–14.

6 The beginning of the end

Joel 2:28–32

We have been with Joel's people through difficult and yet momentous days. Their land had been devastated, their economy ruined. But we have also accompanied them through repentance into blessing again. In our last section their future seemed rosy. But in all their experiences Joel had remined them that both their troubles and their blessings were a minor rehearsal for a bigger crisis of blessing and judgment yet to come. This would be associated, as we have seen, with the Day of the Lord.

The passage we are now looking at forms a kind of bridge between the local disaster and deliverance of the locust plague, and the great final blessing and judgment of mankind by God. The latter will involve God's supreme blessing of man through the outpouring of his Spirit. But it will also involve international upheavals and judgments—even cosmic disasters involving the sun, the moon and the stars. And, in the midst of this great finale, God will be saving those who turn to him and put their trust in him.

Spiritual downpour (2:28–29)

God has *already* poured out a blessing on his people. The good rain has revitalised the earth and thus given them produce as a wonderful token of his love and care. But there is more to come. 'Afterward' (2:28) there will be a downpour of God's Spirit, i.e. God will give himself to men in a new and intimate way. There can be no greater gift than this.

Throughout much of the Old Testament there is a kind of *aristocracy* of the Spirit. Apart from his general activity of maintaining the creation (Genesis 1:2; Job 12:10) and recreating (Ezekiel 37:9,14) the broken spirits of sinful men, God's Spirit seemed to concentrate on special men who were called to special tasks at special times. He rested on judges (Judges 6:34), kings (1 Samuel 16:13) and prophets (Isaiah 61:1), and he empowered men who had special gifts and abilities (Genesis 41:38; Exodus 31:3).

Moses had once longed wistfully that all God's people would be as inspired with the Spirit as were these special people (Numbers 11:26–29). And the same hope is found elsewhere in the Old Testament (Isaiah 44:3; Zechariah 12:10). For example, Ezekiel foresaw the day when hearts would be softened by the Spirit to make them inwardly obedient to God's laws (Ezekiel 36:26–27). A similar prophecy of Jeremiah (Jeremiah 31:31–34) adds that this will bring all God's people into a more intimate personal knowledge of him.

In contrast to this Joel says the gift of God's Spirit will be *democratic*. He will come down upon 'all flesh' regardless of age, sex or status. Old or young (2:28), male or female, slave or free (2:29)—they will all have the same intimacy with God that prophets and other *special* people had. Their 'visions' and 'dreams' will be evidence of this for the men of those days looked upon such things as the distinctive mark of the prophet (Numbers 12:6).

To the first Christians there was no doubt at all that the gift of the Spirit which they received on the day of Pentecost was the fulfilment of this promise. Peter identified it as such by quoting this passage (Acts 2:17–18). John the Baptist had said that Jesus would baptise men with the Spirit (Luke 3:16) just as he himself had baptised with water. Knowing how essential this new baptism was

(John 7:39), Jesus had ordered his disciples to wait in Jerusalem (Acts 1:4–5). The dramatic events of the day of Pentecost were convincing proof that the Spirit had come and that Old Testament prophecies such as Joel's were at last fulfilled. As Peter explained to the crowd the risen Jesus, now exalted to God's right hand, had received from his Father the promise of the Spirit (Acts 2:33) and 'poured out' his presence on his disciples.

Dismantle the world (2:30–32)

But Joel did not see only bright and happy things ahead. He saw terrible warning signs (2:30) on earth and in the sky. Signs were the marks of a true prophet (Deuteronomy 18:21–22; cf. 13:1–3) and evidence that God was intervening in history. At the Exodus (Deuteronomy 26:8), for example, God gave signs like the blood, fire and smoke that Joel describes. The locusts had been a sign of the coming judgment, but they had been only local and earthly. Now Joel gives signs that extend even into the heavens (2:31). This time there will be violence and destruction, and the very earth itself will go up in smoke.

As we have seen (chapter 2) the Day of the Lord is the transition point between this old world, spoiled as it is by sin and death, and God's glorious new age of peace and righteousness. The out-pouring of the Spirit is the sign that the change-over has begun (Romans 8:23). But before the new creation can be completed, the old one must be dismantled. For that reason the day is 'great and terrible' (2:31).

When the world's great final crisis comes, there will be deliverance for escapees and survivors who call upon the name of the Lord. Though God's Spirit has been poured out on all flesh, his salvation is by no means inevitable. It must be personally received by those who respond to his leading and cast themselves upon him and his mercy. They alone will survive the disaster.

Some people may have been surprised that, on the day of Pentecost, Peter not only quoted Joel's prophecy about the Holy Spirit—he also included these verses about the end of the world. In fact Joel's word 'afterwards' really means much the same as 'the last days' (compare 2:28 with Acts 2:17). Why? As far as Peter was concerned the outpouring of the Spirit was the sign that the Day of the Lord had *already* come. Jesus Christ was enthroned as Lord of history and the church, the powers of heaven were already at work and the rest of the world's time schedule was in the hand of God. The last days had already begun.

What a privilege it is for us to live in the last days. How crucial and critical they are! No matter how ordinary or insignificant we may feel, we can have confidence about the future. Once we call upon the name of the Lord Jesus for deliverance from sin and guilt, he baptises us with his Spirit and confers on us the same intimacy that was once limited to the spiritual aristocrats of old. Though we, like all people, must face the crisis of the last judgment, we shall survive it. More than that we shall be citizens of a new and glorious world. What a privilege and a responsibility.

Talking points

1. After reading John 3:5–8 and Ephesians 1:13–14, discuss the role of the Holy Spirit in salvation.

2. Jesus Christ initiates us once and for all into his body, the church, by baptising us with his Spirit. When does this occur, who is it for and what is its purpose? The following passages should prove helpful: Matthew 3:11; 1 Corinthians 12:13; Galatians 3:27. Also, compare Acts 1:4–5 with Acts 2:4.

3. What does being 'filled with the Spirit' mean? Is it an event or a process? What effect does being 'filled with the Spirit' have on the way you live? See Ephesians 5:18–21, John 7:37–39, Acts 2:4 and 4:31.

4. How could Peter justify quoting the whole of Joel 2:38–32 in Acts 2:17–21? Where do the terrifying signs—blood, fire and smoke—fit in? How could Peter say the 'last days' have come when he lived nearly 2000 years ago?

5. Joel 2:32 says that anyone who 'calls on the name of the Lord will be saved'. What does it mean to 'call on the name of the Lord'? What is the relationship between salvation and the 'name of the Lord'? See also Acts 4:12 and 1 John 3:23–24.

7 Showdown with God

Joel 3:1–21

What will happen as the world comes to an end? Does the Bible tell us? Does it give us a detailed schedule of the last events? Some have thought so and have used the Bible almost as a crystal ball. Does Joel do that in this last chapter? Can we use it to foretell the future?

How sin works (3:1–8)

Joel continues to speak of God's final blessing and judgment of the world. But he does it in a way which was relevant to the men who *first* heard him. In our day we must listen to the message behind what he says and not get bogged down in trying to guess when and how it all happens. The *principles*, and not the people or places, are what is important.

On God's day he will not only establish his people as citizens of his new creation (3:1)—he will bring this world's nations into the courtroom for judgment (3:2). The 'valley of Jehoshaphat' may refer to an actual place (it has been identified as the Valley of Kidron), but it may also be symbolic. Valleys in the Old Testament figure in pictures of final judgment (Ezekiel 39:11; Zechariah 14:4ff) and the name 'Jehoshaphat', though that of a former Judaean king (2 Chronicles 20:1–30), means 'the Lord judges'. The nations will be judged for the inhumanity that they have shown to God's people and thus to God himself (see also 3:12,14).

For all sin is ultimately against God. The Phoenicians of Tyre and Sidon and Israel's old enemies from Philistia (3:4) thought that when they sold up God's land and its people they were dealing only with men. But they were in fact 'paying God back'. Their crime would rebound on their own heads. They stole Judaean wealth (3:5) but it belonged to God. They sold God's people into slavery (3:6), but they would not only be returned (3:7)—they would sell off these people-sellers themselves (3:8).

For one thing we can be sure of is that on the day of judgment men will realise that all sin is against God. Every act of inhumanity is an assault on him. And all sin sets up a reaction which eventually recoils on the sinner.

The final verdict (3:9–15)

God summons mankind to a showdown. He sends the call to war (3:9) to the nations. Let them ready themselves. Let them collect all the weapons they can and summon every available soldier (3:10). Let them gather for battle against the Lord's warriors (3:11)—the heavenly hosts, the real defenders of Israel (2 Kings 6:16–17). But as they come to the *battleground* they will find in fact that they are in the valley *courtroom* (3:12, see also 3:2) where God sits in judgment! There they will realise that their opposition to his people and their witness is really a rejection of him and his claims. The case against mankind is not that they fight against God's people but against God himself. And so great is *this* wickedness that the harvest of world judgment (3:13) must begin (Isaiah 17:5, Matthew 13:39; Revelation 14:14–20).

In history the age-old battle between good and evil goes on. Everybody, at some time or other, wonders if it will ever end. There never seems to be any conclusion to it, nor any final decision. But, says Joel, on the Day of the Lord there will be. He describes the noise and confusion of all mankind (3:14), gathered together in that 'valley'—the symbol not only of their struggle against God, but also of his judgment of their case. The showdown is near, says Joel, when God will hand down his final verdict against evil and all who oppose him. He will dismantle the world as the signs in the sky show (3:15) and he will make his final assessment of individuals and groups in history.

On that day God alone will make the decision. And yet, in a sense, we also make them. For God's decision will partly be based on the decisions which we make *now*. We will be on trial for our attitudes to God and the salvation which he offers us in Christ. We will be assessed on whether we are at war with him, or whether we have submitted to his grace and control. From this point of view then, we are living now in the 'valley of decision'. Where do we stand—with God or against him? There is no middle ground.

The world remade (3:16–21)

The vast locust swarm once looked as if it would be the end of Joel's nation. But by God's grace his penitent people survived and their land became fruitful again. It will be like that on the Day of the Lord. When God dismantles the world, those who have called upon him will survive. And, better than that, they will enter into a blessedness richer and more enduring than anything they have ever known.

When the universe shakes and falls apart, God will be a refuge and stronghold (3:16b) to his people. He will roar (3:16a) at all that would destroy them and thus assure them that he is personally amongst them (3:17a).

The Last Judgment will purify the whole creation. It will remove all evil 'foreign bodies' and set up a truly holy society or city (3:17b). This will be, of course, beyond the end of history. The best commentary on it is the Book of Revelation (Revelation 21–22). There we see the *new* Jerusalem, God's own city, where his holy presence makes it impossible for anything sad or evil (Revelation 21:8,27) ever to exist again.

The end of the world will spell the end of all cruel worldly powers, as illustrated by Israel's ancient enemies Edom and Egypt (3:19,21a). Their desolation will be the dark background to the blessedness of God's new society, which by contrast is safe and secured (3:20).

And what a blessed world it will be! Joel describes it in terms of fertility and fruitfulness somewhat as he did after the locust plague (2:24) but more so. He sees the creation, with sin and evil removed, now reach its glorious potential (Romans 8:19–23). Wine, milk and water (3:18) are the symbols of its blessedness. Especially water, for in that dry area it was a constant picture of future blessedness (see Ezekiel 47:1–12 and Zechariah 14:8–9). Like the river which flowed out of Paradise (Genesis 2:10; Revelation 22:1–2) it will bring life, vitality, health and fruitfulness—even in the notably dry and unreliable gullies like Shittim ('acacias', NIV).

A world remade. A world without tears, sin or death. *This* is what lies before us. Beyond the holocaust of judgment and the falling debris of a world destroyed is a land and a city of unbelievable beauty and joy. And the secret of being part of it is the secret of the Christian life now—having the Lord Jesus dwell in us (3:21b) as Saviour and Lord.

Talking points

1. Read Job 25:4, Psalm 51:4, Ecclesiastes 7:29, Romans 3:9–10 and 1 John 1:8–9. What does each of these passages have to say about sin? What does this tell you about our own sinfulness? How should you respond to this knowledge?

2. What are God's criteria for judgment? See Matthew 7:21, 25:31–46 and Romans 2:5–8.
   Where does faith fit into all this? See Romans 4:1–5 and Galatians 3:11.

3. The Old Testament prophets often show God judging nations (e.g. Joel 3:1–16). Does God still judge nations today? How would you know that a national setback (e.g. natural disaster) was God's specific judgment and not simply the logical outcome of living in a fallen world?

4. Is it wrong to hope or pray for divine retribution against ungodly individuals or nations? In your discussion compare Matthew 5:43–45 with Hebrews 10:30–31. See also Joel 3:21 and Revelation 6:9–10.

5. Highlight briefly the main lesson (or lessons) you have learnt from your study of the book of Joel. How can you apply this lesson to your life?

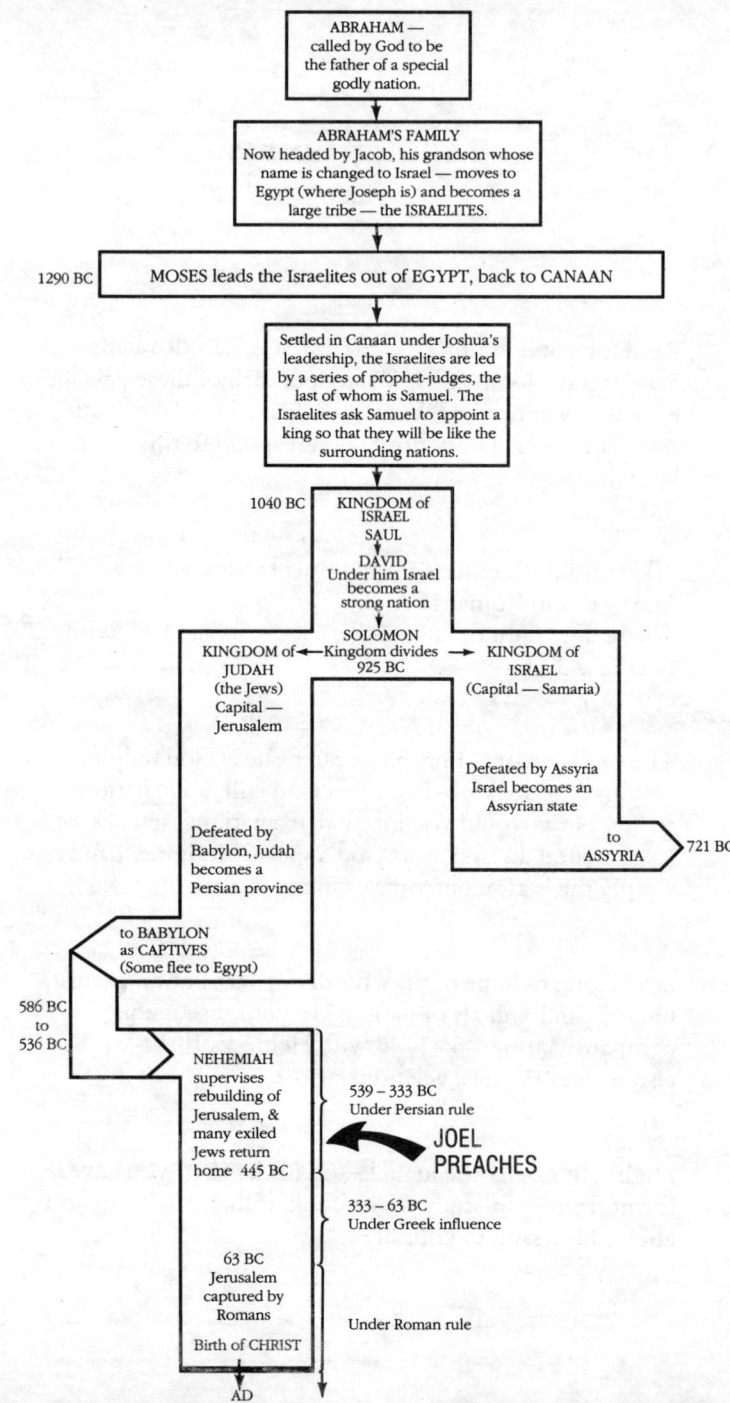